AMERICA AND THE AMERICANS

The Erie Canal

Wagon Wheels

Molly's Pilgrim

John Henry

The Girl Who Loved Wild Horses

Why Don't You Get a Horse, Sam Adams?

Literature-Based Reading Activities

Written by Linda Ward Beech, Tara McCarthy, and Eleanor Ripp
Text illustrated by Claude Martinot
Cover illustrated by Jane Conteh-Morgan

Newbridge Educational Programs

Acknowledgments

IIllustrations from The *Erie Canal,* written and illustrated by Peter Spier. Illustrations copyright © 1970 by Peter Spier. Reprinted by permission of Doubleday.

Illustrations from *Wagon Wheels* by Barbara Brenner. Illustrated by Don Bolognese. Illustrations copyright © 1978 by Don Bolognese. Reprinted by permission of HarperCollins.

Illustrations from *Molly's Pilgrim,* by Barbara Cohen. Illustrated by Michael J. Deraney. Illustrations copyright © 1983 by Michael J. Deraney. Reprinted by permission of William Morrow and Company.

Illustrations from *John Henry,* written and illustrated by Ezra Jack Keats. Illustrations copyright © 1965 by Ezra Jack Keats. Reprinted by permission of The Ezra Jack Keats Foundation.

Illustrations from *The Girl Who Loved Wild Horses,* written and illustrated by Paul Goble. Illustrati.ons copyright © 1978 by Paul Goble. Reprinted by permission of Bradbury Press, a division of Macmilllian Publishing.

Illustrations from *Why Don't You Get a Horse, Sam Adams?* by Jean Fritz. Illustrated by Trina Schart Hyman. Illustrations copyright © 1974 by Trina Schart Hyman. Reprinted by permission of Coward-McCann, Inc.

AMERICA AND THE AMERICANS
Table of Contents

continued

Table of Contents (Continued)

PRE-READING ACTIVITIES

Meet the Author: Peter Spier
Born in Amsterdam, the Netherlands, on June 6, 1927, Peter Edward Spier grew up in Broek-in-Waterland, a small Dutch village. The Spier house was on the water, and boats passed by daily, perhaps accounting for Spier's later artistic interest in them. Spier's father was a famous political cartoonist, and at the age of 18, Spier decided that he, too, would be an artist. His first job was in the Paris office of a Dutch weekly newspaper. Later, Spier was transferred to Houston, Texas. From there, he made his way to New York City and became a freelance artist.

Spier illustrated about fifty books by other people before writing his own. In 1978 he won the Caldecott Medal for his book *Noah's Ark*. As a result, his father gave him a collection of works by Randolph Caldecott, including many first editions. The pages that Peter Spier had colored red as a three-year-old still had the crayon marks on them!

Spier spends considerable time researching his books. For *The Erie Canal* he drove the full length of the canal twice. He made sketches on these trips, then put them together to create a book when he returned home.

Story Summary In song and pictures this book tells the story of the Erie Canal, begun in 1817 and completed in 1825. The song follows the path of an Erie Canal barge worker, or "hoggee," and his mule as they pull the barge through the canal. Spier's richly detailed illustrations show the traffic and life along the canal, including landscapes, towns, cargo, and people. The words to the popular song provide the text. The back of the book also includes a map and historical background about the canal. Such intriguing

questions as "What did canal children do?" and "How many animals pulled a boat?" are carefully answered. Finally, the book includes the music to the song so that readers can really sing the text as they turn the colorful pages.

Building Background Write the word *canal* on the chalkboard, and call on volunteers to explain what it means. Ask another volunteer to look up the word in a dictionary. Guide students in understanding that a canal is an artificial waterway or channel. Then ask students to think about why people would build a canal. Write their ideas on the board, then circle the ones that apply to the Erie Canal. Point out that long ago there were no cars and few roads, so it was often easier to travel by water than by land. Tell students that they will be reading about a very famous canal built more than 150 years ago. Ask them to look and listen to find out what made the boats and barges on this canal move.

Hum a Little Tune If students don't already know the song about the Erie Canal, teach them the tune. Once the class has mastered the song and the chorus, explain that the words in the book go with the tune. On a second reading of the book, ask the class to softly hum each line of the song as you read the words.

The Erie Canal
Comprehension

Name _____

Erie Information

Answer each question below in a complete sentence. The clues in the barges will help you.

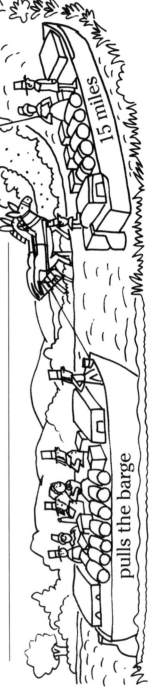

the Erie Canal

a mule

15 miles

people and cargo

pulls the barge

1. What is the song about? _____

2. Who is Sal? _____

3. What does Sal do? _____

4. What does the barge carry? _____

5. How many miles does Sal go each day? _____

• What does everyone do when they come to a low bridge? _____

The Erie Canal
Vocabulary: Rhyming Words

Name _____

Sal's Canal

When you hear the words to the song, you hear rhyming words. Write the word from the barrel that rhymes with the underlined word in each sentence below.

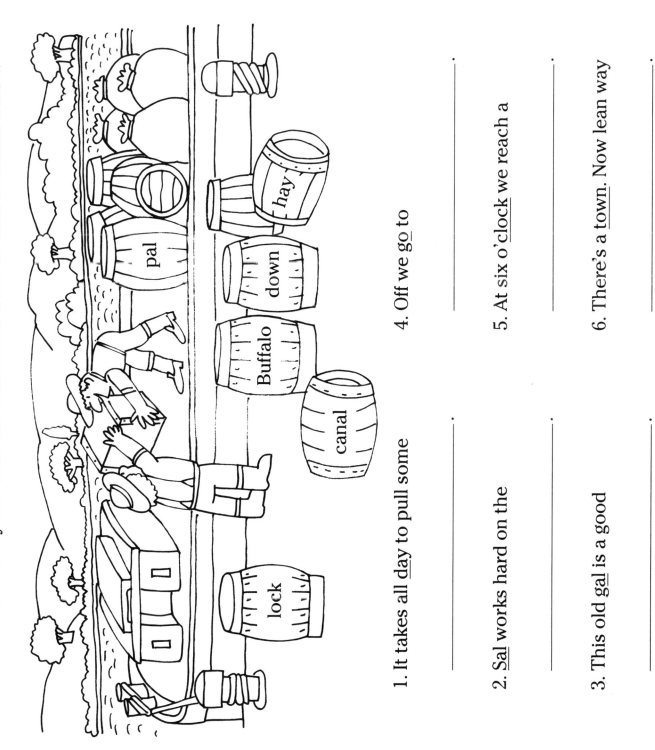

1. It takes all day to pull some _____

2. Sal works hard on the _____

3. This old gal is a good _____

4. Off we go to _____

5. At six o'clock we reach a _____

6. There's a town. Now lean way _____

- On the back of this page use one pair of rhyming words in a sentence of your own.

The Erie Canal
Story Structure: Setting

Name _____

On the Map

Study the map. Then follow the directions.

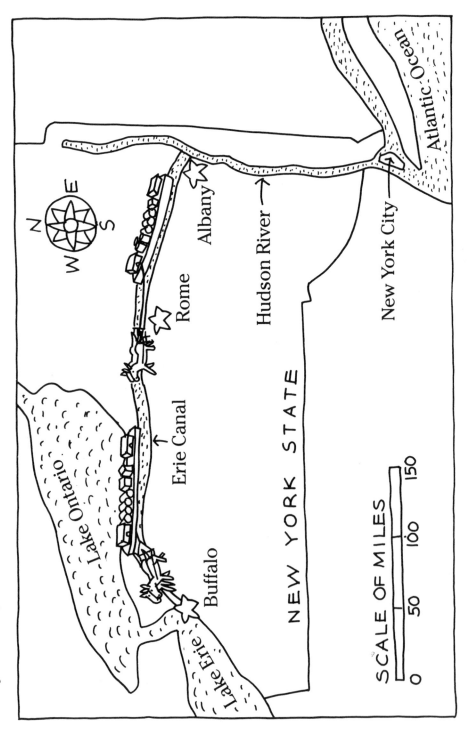

1. Find and underline the city of Buffalo.

2. Find and circle the city of Albany.

3. Find Lake Erie. Color it blue.

4. Draw a blue line along the Erie Canal from Buffalo to Albany.

5. Write the name of the river that links up with the Erie Canal.

   _____

● In what state is the Erie Canal?

Meet a Mule

Suppose you could ask Sal these questions. What do you think she would say? Write her answers in complete sentences on the lines.

What do you see on your trips?

Sal: _____
_____
_____
_____

What towns do you pass through?

Sal: _____
_____

Why is your job important?

Sal: _____
_____

What is the best part of your job?

Sal: _____

• On the back of this page write another question that you might ask Sal.

Art/Oral Language Activity

MOVING RIGHT ALONG

Barge-o-Rama In this activity, students will re-create a trip along the Erie Canal.

You need:

shoe boxes	pencils or small wooden rods	scissors
colored markers	a roll of calculator paper	
barge pattern	mule pattern	glue

Steps:

1. Ask students to bring to class shoe boxes or boxes of similar shape. (Lids are not needed.) Help students cut a 4-inch slit on either end of the box, about 1 inch from the box bottom as shown.

2. Provide each student with a length of calculator paper. Invite them to draw some of the different towns, landscapes, and other scenes that the barge passes on its trip along the Erie Canal. Allow students to consult the book for ideas or to use their own imaginations.

3. Show students how to glue one end of their barge-o-rama scrolls around a pencil to roll it up. Show them how to slip the open end of the scroll through both slits so it is stretched across the back of the shoe box.

4. Tell students to glue and roll the open end of the scroll around a second pencil. Demonstrate how students can make the background change for the barge trip by turning the pencils.

5. Reproduce the barge and mule patterns on this page and provide copies for each student. Have students color their patterns.

6. Have students fold down the tabs at the bottom of the barge and mule and glue them to the bottom of the open box. The barge should be near the front with the mule slightly ahead and to the side of it.

Barge-o-Rama Drama Invite students to share their barge-o-ramas with the class. As a student turns the background scroll, he or she can describe the passing scene. Encourage students to sing the Erie Canal song along with their barge-o-ramas.

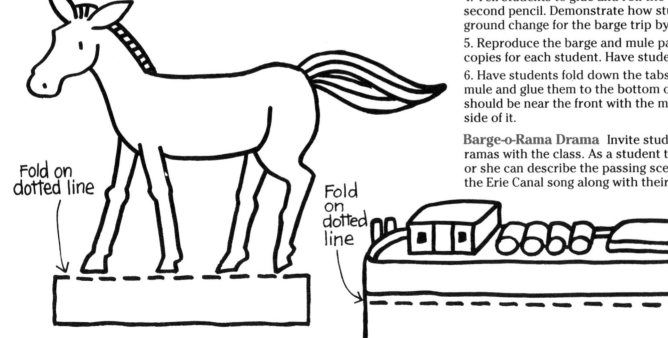

Fold on dotted line

Fold on dotted line

Cooperative Learning/Listening/Speaking

WORDS AND MUSIC

Sing and Swing Once students know the words and tune to the Erie Canal song, try one or more of these activities with them.

• Have the class start by singing the first lines of the song very softly, the second lines just a little more loudly, and the next lines more loudly still, until the last word of the song–*Buffalo*–is boomed out. Repeat the pattern with the chorus, again ending on a loud note.

• Divide the class into five groups and sing the chorus as a round. Explain that in a round each group starts singing at a different time. Tell students that they must all watch you, the conductor, to know when each group should start the first line. Remind students to listen carefully only to the members of their group because it is easy to get mixed up. Practice with the class until you complete one full round of the chorus.

• Have students work in groups to make up motions to use with each line of the song. Assign two groups to work on the first verse, two on the second verse, and two groups on the chorus. After students have had time to practice their movements, invite each group to sing and perform for the class. Then try putting the whole song together. Discuss how groups came up with different actions for the same parts of the song.

• Challenge students to tap or clap out the beat as the song is sung or played. Clappers use their hands, while tappers might use pencils, rulers, or paintbrushes.

• Invite students who play a musical instrument to learn the music included in the book. Ask your "band" to play as the rest of the class sings the song.

• Challenge students to work with a partner or in small groups to write another verse to the song. Invite students to teach their new verses to the class.

Cycle of Seasons Divide the class into four groups. Assign each group one of the four seasons. Explain that the book shows four pictures of the same place along the canal in the different seasons. These illustrations are on the first two pages and the last two pages of the book. Give each group a large sheet of poster paper with its season labeled on top. Then ask students to study the picture of its season and to make notes and draw pictures on the poster paper about life along the canal during that time of year. Give students the following guiding questions to work with:

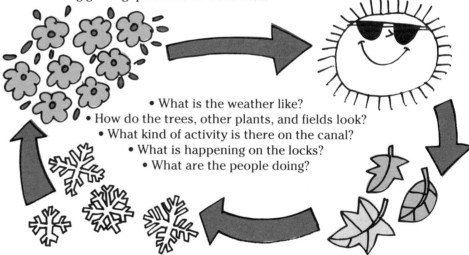

• What is the weather like?
• How do the trees, other plants, and fields look?
• What kind of activity is there on the canal?
• What is happening on the locks?
• What are the people doing?

Ask each group to share its observations. Display the completed posters side by side so students can see how the cycle of seasons affected life on the canal. Point out that a cold winter caused the canal to shut down. Guide students in thinking about what this meant in terms of transporting cargo and people across the state and to and from farther west.

EXTENDED ACTIVITIES

Creative Writing: On the Canal Point out to students that there are many children in Peter Spier's illustrations of canal boats and packets. Ask students to think about what it would be like to live on a canal boat. Then have students write a journal entry for a day in the life of a child living on the canal.

Visual Literacy: Detective Work Help students appreciate the rich details in the book's illustrations with this activity. Write questions like the following on slips of paper. Place the questions in an envelope, and invite students to pick a question and try to find the answer in the pictures.

- How did people catch fish in the canal in winter?
  (They dug a hole in the ice.)
- Name two foods that the mules ate.
  (oats and carrots)
- Find the name of a barge.
  (*Small Hope, Bumble Bee, Star, Annie, Bridget, Benjamin H. Cooper*)
- How did people wash and dry their clothes on a barge?
  (They washed them in a tub and hung them on a line up top.)
- What was the fine for driving on the towpath?
  ($5.00)
- What kinds of containers were used to hold the cargo?
  (barrels, sacks, crates)

- Name some ways that people traveled on land along the canal. (horse-drawn sled or carriage; wagon pulled by oxen; on foot; on horseback; by bicycle)

Find the Facts As a culminating activity, turn to the historical notes at the back of the book. Read the first paragraph aloud to the class, stopping to identify the place names on a map of New York state. Clarify that via the Hudson River, the canal connected New York City and the Atlantic Ocean with Buffalo and the Great Lakes, a journey of about 550 miles. At this time it was far faster and cheaper to ship farm products and raw materials by water than over land. Ask students to answer these questions: Did the Erie Canal contribute to the growth of towns and cities along its route? How?

Before reading the second paragraph, write each of the 14 italicized questions featured in it on the chalkboard. Tell students that you are going to give them more background information about the Erie Canal. Explain that when you come to each question, you will point to it on the board, and students should listen carefully for the answer. Later, invite interested students who have additional questions to do further research and to report back to the class. A good source for students is the October, 1982, issue of *Cobblestone: The History Magazine for Young*

People. If copies are not available in your local library, they can be ordered by writing to: Cobblestone Publishing, Inc., 30 Grove Street, Peterborough, NH 03458. Single back issues cost $3.95.

Reading: Peter's Pictures If students enjoyed this book by Peter Spier, introduce them to some of his other titles: *The Star-Spangled Banner, The Legend of New Amsterdam, Tin Lizzie,* and his 1978 Caldecott winner, *Noah's Ark.* Invite students to report to the class about one of these titles that they would recommend. Then post their reports in a "Critics' Corner" in your reading center.

PRE-READING ACTIVITIES

Meet the Author: Barbara Brenner Born in Brooklyn, New York, on June 26, 1925, Barbara Brenner began her writing career at the age of 25. Some of the nearly 50 books she has written include *A Snake-Lover's Diary* and *A Year in the Life of Rosie Bernard*. Her years as a writer-consultant and instructor at Bank Street College of Education helped her focus on urban children and on literature for minority groups. *Wagon Wheels*, which was selected as an American Library Association Notable Book in 1978, is a result of these interests.

Brenner has also written extensively about the world of nature. Five of her science books for children, including *Baltimore Orioles*, won awards from the National Science Teachers Association and the Children's Book Council. She enjoys bird watching, fossil hunting, yoga, and organic gardening.

Meet the Artist: Don Bolognese In addition to illustrating over 150 books, Don Bolognese has written children's books and is a well-known painter, calligrapher, and graphic designer. He has taught at various art schools, including the Metropolitan Museum of Art's medieval museum, the Cloisters. Bolognese was born in New York City on January 6, 1934.

Story Summary *Wagon Wheels* is the true story of the Muldies, a black pioneer family that settled in Nicodemus, Kansas, in 1878. The trip has been a difficult one for Ed Muldie and his three young sons, for the children's mother has died along the way. Now the family must face the difficulties of life on the prairie. Their home is merely a hole in the ground–dirt floors and walls, a grass roof, and no windows. The family's food supply is desperately low during the freezing winter, but they, like others in the community, are saved by the Osage Indians, who leave them meat, vegetables, and fuel. In the spring, Ed Muldie leaves his sons to search for a better place for the family to settle. The boys must be even braver and more responsible than before as they wait for their father to send for them. They hunt, fish, cook, and clean, and the two older boys keep a careful watch over their three-year-old brother.

When their father's letter arrives three months later, the boys leave the next day to join him. They travel on foot over 150 miles, living among wild animals for nearly a month. Finally they reach their father and begin a new life.

Land of the Free Provide some background by explaining to students that in order for people to own land today, they must buy it. However, when the Muldies went West, they didn't have to pay any money at all for land. In those days, there was a law that gave land to people for free. The Homestead Act of 1862 granted 160-acre tracts of public land to any head of a family who would live on the land for five years and improve it. Men, such as Ed Muldie, had an opportunity to own land they otherwise could not afford. The last page of *Wagon Wheels* provides further information on the background of this true story.

Wagon Wheels
Comprehension

Going West

Name _____

Name _____

Each chapter of *Wagon Wheels* tells a different part of the story. Write a sentence that tells something important that happens in each chapter.

Chapter I: The Dugout _____

_____

_____

Chapter II: Indians _____

_____

_____

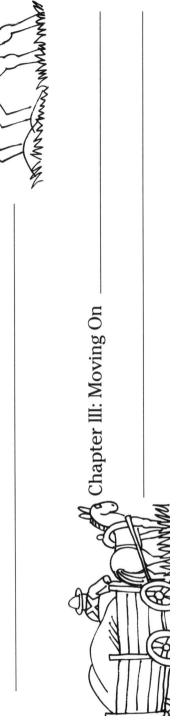

Chapter III: Moving On _____

_____

_____

Chapter IV: The Letter _____

_____

_____

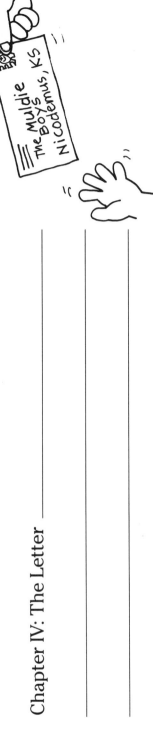

• Circle the chapter you like best. On the back of the page draw a picture of something that happens in that chapter.

Wagon Wheels
Vocabulary

Wagon-Wheel Words

Help tell the story of *Wagon Wheels*. Choose a word from the wagon to complete each sentence.

Name _____

firewood

cornmeal

dugout

rattlesnake

saddlebags

1. In Nicodemus the Muldies live in a _____ .

2. For most of the winter, the only food the family has to eat is mush made from _____ .

3. No one in Nicodemus has any _____ to burn.

4. The Indians carry food and sticks in their _____ .

5. One night the boys see a big prairie _____ .

• Add the correct word to complete this sentence.

A _____ brings a letter to the boys.

Name _____

Wagon Wheels
Story Structure: Sequence

The Way West

Each sentence below tells about the story, but in the wrong order. Write a number from 1 to 6 in each picture to show the right order.

☐ The boys get a letter from their father.

☐ The family builds a dugout.

☐ Ed Muldie leaves to find land with trees and hills.

☐ The boys and their father arrive in Nicodemus.

☐ The boys leave Nicodemus to join their father.

☐ The boys find their father.

● What do you think might happen next to the Muldies? Write your ideas on the back of this page.

Wagon Wheels
Creative Writing

Name _____

On the Prairie

Pretend you are Johnny Muldie. You keep a diary telling about your trip to join your father. Fill in your diary for the days below.

Day 1: Getting Started _____

_____

_____

Day 8: A Scary Time _____

_____

_____

_____

_____

Day 22: Almost There _____

_____

_____

• On the back of the page draw a picture to go with one of your diary entries.

AT HOME ON THE PRAIRIE

Wagon-Wheels Mural Let students create this mural to recall the things the pioneers took with them when they went west.

You need:

a long sheet of mural paper	sketch paper
a black marker pencils regular or oil crayons tape	

Steps:

1. Ahead of time, title the mural paper A WAGON FULL OF WONDERS in black marker. Then draw the outline of a large wagon.

2. Discuss the kinds of belongings and supplies that pioneers like the Muldies might have brought with them in their wagons going west. Reread and carefully study with the class the book illustrations to find some of the Muldies' belongings. Ask students what they think the purpose of each was. Also discuss and list additional items that pioneers might have brought with them: bags of seed, clock, rope, hammer, cloth, plow, ax, candles, kettle, tin pitcher, matches, match bottle (to keep matches dry), crosscut saw.

3. Have each student choose an object to sketch in pencil. (There should be enough objects for each student.)

4. Now securely tape the prepared mural paper on a wall where it is low enough for children to reach easily.

5. Then have students take turns drawing their sketches in regular or oil crayons inside the wagon outline. (Suggest that students use light colors before darker ones as oil crayons smudge.)

6. When the mural is complete, use a dark oil crayon to highlight the title. Display the finished mural in a prominent place, and invite other classes to view it. Encourage students to explain the parts they worked on.

Dugout Diorama In this activity students can re-create life in a prairie dugout.

You need:

scissors	crayons	glue	construction paper
	tape	woolen scraps	
small twigs		cotton	green crepe paper

Steps:

1. Discuss what the Muldies kept in their dugout. Show students the pictures on pages 17 and 29 that show a kerosene lamp, barrel, wooden table, spoons, bowls, and banjo.

2. Then provide students with oaktag, and have them draw and cut out a dugout shape like the one on this page.

3. Have students draw an interior scene on their dugout shapes. Suggest that they include the tools and furniture mentioned in the story.

4. Show students how to fold the dugout on each side so it stands up. Have students fold it across the top to create a roof.

5. For extra touches, have students glue green crepe-paper grass and twigs to the top of the dugout. For firewood, they might tape tiny bundles of twigs or toothpicks together. For blankets, they can cut out woolen scraps, and for smoke coming from the roof, they might stuff a small piece of cotton through the top of the dugout.

6. Encourage students to draw and tape figures to the dugout.

Cooperative Learning/Listening/Speaking

DUGOUT PARTY

Hold a class dugout party so students can experience the way the Muldies might enjoy themselves in Nicodemus. Start the activity by asking students what they do in their spare time (watch TV, play video games, play softball, listen to records). Ask the class if they think the Muldies did these activities too. Why or why not? Point out that back then, modern entertainment like television, movies, and organized sports did not exist, so families had to keep busy in other ways. Explain that the class will experience these other ways at their Dugout Party.

The Reel Thing Teach this simple square dance to the tune of "Oh, Susanna!" Have boys and girls form separate lines of about 8-10 students each facing each other. Then call out–and clap out–the directions below.

Walk toward each other; bow or curtsy.	(4 counts)
Walk back to your place.	(4 counts)
Repeat.	(8 counts)
Head couple hold hands and skip down the line. Every one clap your hands.	(8 counts)
Head couple hold hands and skip up the line. Then hold hands up like a bridge.	(8 counts)
Other couples walk under bridge, turn around, march down the line, then march back up.	
Head couple follow last couple at end of line.	(16 counts)

Repeat the entire song enough times so each couple gets a chance to be the head couple or as interest holds.

Plain Cookin' Remind students that the Muldie boys baked corn bread when they lived alone. The pioneers often called it *johnnycake* and cooked it on a griddle, like pancakes. Students may wish to prepare this johnnycake recipe in school or at home for the dugout party.

You need:

2 cups of cornmeal	2 eggs	2 cups of milk
3 teaspoons of baking soda		2/3 cup of honey
1 3/4 cups of flour	1 1/2 tablespoons of molasses	
1/2 teaspoon of salt	2 tablespoons of cooking oil	

Steps:

1. Preheat the oven to 425 degrees. Then let students mix the cornmeal, baking soda, flour, and salt together in a bowl.

2. In a second bowl, have students beat the eggs, then add the other ingredients to it.

3. Instruct students to combine all the ingredients into a big bowl and stir. Have them pour the mixture into two 8" x 8" baking pans and bake for 30 minutes. The recipe makes 32 squares.

Wojapi Explain to students that the Osage Indians, who gave food to the starving Muldies, belong to the Sioux nation. At that time, they grew beans, squash, corn, melons, and pumpkin. They also gathered berries. With students, prepare this Sioux recipe. Serve it warm with the corn bread.

You need:

4 pounds of blueberries	
1 cup of flour	1 1/2 cups of water
2 teaspoons of honey	

Steps:

1. Have students place the blueberries and water in a pan and mash them.

2. Instruct students to add the flour and honey and stir.

3. Place the pan on a hot plate, and cook over medium heat, stirring until the wojapi thickens.

4. Serve warm with the corn bread.

EXTENDED ACTIVITIES

Social Studies: Black Heroes of the West

Black men and women played important roles in the development of the West. Interested students can research the lives of these heroes, and groups of students can then dramatize the heroes' adventures for the rest of the class.

Jean Baptiste Point Du Sable: Early fur trapper. He set up a trading post which became the city of Chicago.

James Beckwourth: Famous mountain man who became a Crow Indian chief, he discovered a pass through the Sierra Nevada Mountains, now called the Beckwourth Pass.

Benjamin "Pap" Singleton: In the 1870s, Singleton urged blacks to move to black settlements in Oklahoma and Kansas, including Nicodemus.

Mary Fields: Escaped slavery and settled in Montana, where she became an expert stage driver to deliver the mail.

These two books will provide additional information about the role of blacks in the development of the West: *The Black Frontiersman* by J. Norman Heard and *Exploring Black America* by Marcella Thum.

Tale Telling

Telling stories was a favorite pastime of the pioneers. As a summarizing activity, have students sit in a circle and pretend they are in the dugout. Start a prairie adventure, and let each student add a sentence to it. Some story-starters are: "The night of the terrible prairie fire, we..." "When we heard the snake's tail rattle, we knew that..." and "It was so cold in the dugout, we..." As a follow-up, encourage interested students to write their own prairie adventures to share with others.

Geography: Ed Muldie's Map

Reread pages 46-49 and 56-58 to the class. Then tell students that they, too, can find their way from Nicodemus to Solomon. Display a map of Kansas from an encyclopedia or atlas. Help students locate Nicodemus in the north-central part of the state on Route 24. Point out that the town is near the South Fork Solomon River. Have students trace the river going east and then south until they find Solomon. Conclude by having students draw picture maps, like Mr. Muldie might have drawn for his boys. These maps might include the two towns, the river, deer trail, and perhaps some of the wild animals mentioned in the story. Remind students to add labels for Kansas, the towns, and the river.

Language Arts: What Would Willie Say?

In the book eleven-year-old Johnny tells the story. How would eight-year-old Willie tell it? or three-year-old Little Brother? or old Mrs. Sadler? Invite students to describe one of the following scenes from the point of view of one of these characters. Encourage students to illustrate their stories.

- The Muldies arrive in Nicodemus.
- The Muldies spend a "mean" winter in the dugout.
- The boys live alone.
- The people of Nicodemus escape the prairie fire.
- The boys see the rattlesnake.

Pioneer Post

To summarize *Wagon Wheels*, remind students that a post rider on horseback delivers the letter to the Muldie boys. Ask students to pretend that they, too, are pioneers in Nicodemus and that they are going to send a letter to a friend or relative back home in Kentucky. Have students write about one of the problems the Muldies face on the prairie. Invite students to read their finished letters to the class, then display them on a bulletin board titled PIONEER POST.

PRE-READING ACTIVITIES

Meet the Author: Barbara Cohen Born in New Jersey on March 15, 1932, Barbara Cohen spent her childhood listening to relatives tell stories about each other. From these tales of troubles and joy, she absorbed not only the flavor of times gone by, but also the art

of story-telling. Among her other books are *The Orphan Game, The Christmas Revolution*, and *The Carp in the Bathtub*, considered by some critics to be a modern classic. In 1985, *Molly's Pilgrim* was made into a film. It received the Academy Award for Best Short Film.

Cohen states that she never sets out to write children's books. She merely recounts what is important to her. She is the winner of the 1983 National Jewish Book Award for children's fiction for *Yussel's Prayer*.

Meet the Artist: Michael J. Deraney Michael J. Deraney comes from Grand Forks, North Dakota. Before moving to New York to work full-time as an artist and illustrator, he worked as a special-education resource teacher. Deraney has illustrated such books as Mary Haynes's *Pot Belly Tales* and Barbara Cohen's *Yussel's Prayer*.

Story Summary Molly and her family have fled Russia for a life of freedom in America. First living in New York, but now living in Winter Hill, they look different from everyone else and speak English with an accent. Elizabeth and the other children in Molly's third-grade class taunt her. Only her mother's reminder that America offers them a better life comforts her.

At school one day in November, Molly learns about Thanksgiving. Her teacher asks each student to make a Pilgrim or Indian doll out of a clothespin so the class can re-create the Pilgrim village at Plymouth. Molly's mother offers to make the Pilgrim doll, and she creates a Russian peasant doll in her own image. Molly is worried because her doll looks different from her classmates'. Molly's teacher, however, explains that Molly's beautiful doll is indeed a Pilgrim—a modern Pilgrim, someone who came to America, just as the Pilgrims did long ago, to worship God in her own way.

Mama's Yiddish Explain that in *Molly's Pilgrim*, Molly's mother speaks Yiddish to her. Go over the words that Molly's mother uses by writing the words on the chalkboard and having children practice saying them. For an added challenge, invite students to translate into Yiddish the following sentences.

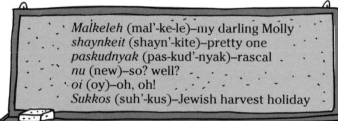

Malkeleh (mal'-ke-le)–my darling Molly
shaynkeit (shayn'-kite)–pretty one
paskudnyak (pas-kud'-nyak)–rascal
nu (new)–so? well?
oi (oy)–oh, oh!
Sukkos (suh'-kus)–Jewish harvest holiday

- So, my darling Molly, where is the (*veer ist der*) rascal? (*Nu, Malkeleh, veer ist der paskudnyak?*)
- Pretty one, when is (*ven ist*) the Jewish harvest festival? (*Shaynkeit, ven ist Sukkos?*)

Let's Meet the Pilgrims Review with students what they know about the Pilgrims and the first Thanksgiving at Plymouth. Ask students to recall what the Pilgrims looked like. Next hold up *Molly's Pilgrim*, and point to the Pilgrim doll on the cover. Ask students why they think this Pilgrim doll looks so different from their ideas of the traditional Pilgrim. Record students' responses, and after reading the book, have them check to see how close they came to the correct answer.

Molly's Pilgrim
Comprehension

Name _____

Jolly Molly

Read each sentence about Molly's feelings. Color the doll yellow if the sentence is true. Color the doll blue if the sentence is false.

1. At first Molly likes the school in Winter Hill.

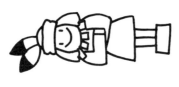

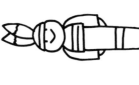

2. Molly feels different from the other children.

3. Molly is upset that Elizabeth makes fun of her.

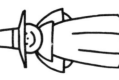

4. Molly is proud of Mama's accent.

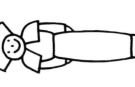

5. Molly is worried that Miss Stickley will not like her doll.

6. At the end, Molly is sad because Thanksgiving turns out to be a terrible holiday for her.

• Is "Jolly Molly" a good name for Molly? On the back of the page write why or why not.

Molly's Pilgrim
Vocabulary

Molly's Bulletin Board

Complete each sentence about Molly with a word from the paper strip.

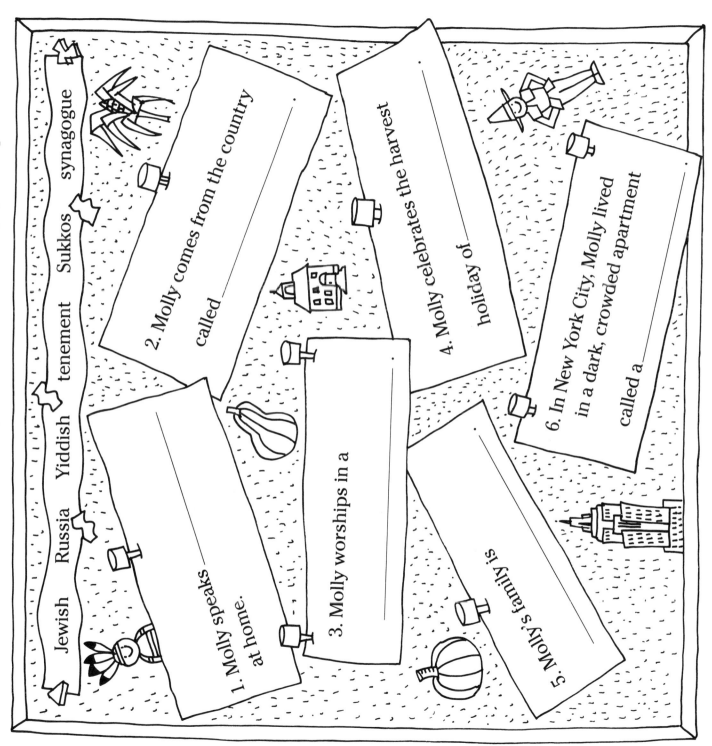

Jewish   Russia   Yiddish   tenement   Sukkos   synagogue

1. Molly speaks _____ at home.

2. Molly comes from the country called _____

3. Molly worships in a _____

4. Molly celebrates the harvest holiday of _____

5. Molly's family is _____

6. In New York City, Molly lived in a dark, crowded apartment called a _____

● On the line write the name of the town in Russia that Molly's family comes from. _____

Molly's Pilgrim
Story Structure: Setting

Name _____

A Home for Molly

Molly has lived in three places. On the lines write the sentences that describe each place.

She lives in a tenement.

She lives in a nice apartment.

She cannot go to school.

She is afraid of the Cossacks.

Her father works in a factory.

She speaks differently from the other children.

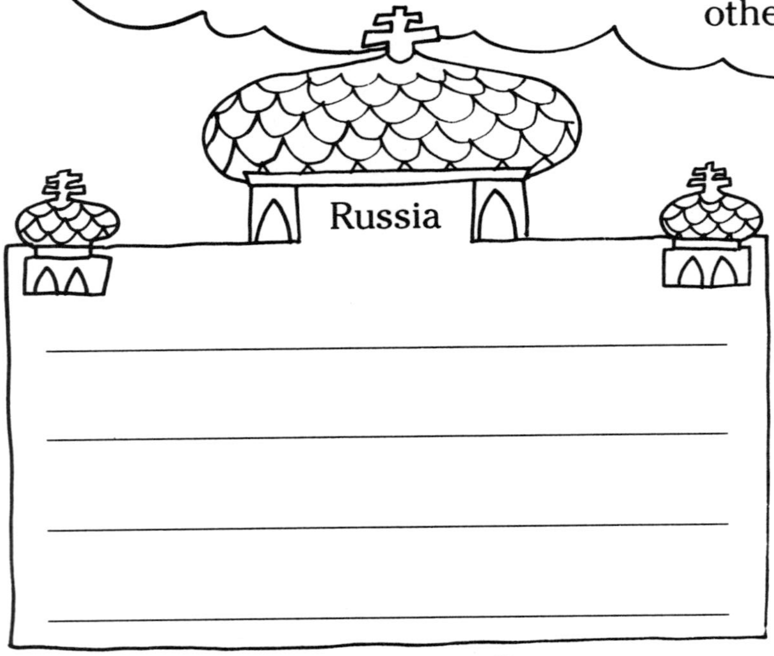

New York City

Russia

Winter Hill

• In which two places do Molly and her family find freedom?

Molly's Pilgrim
Creative Writing

What a Difference a Year Makes

Pretend you are Molly one year later, and it is Thanksgiving again. Complete the
story below.

Name _____

Now I am in the fourth grade. This Thanksgiving _____

_____

Some of my friends are _____

_____

The friend I like best is _____

_____ because

_____

Elizabeth and I _____

_____

I think Winter Hill is _____

_____ because

• On the back of the page draw a picture for your story.

Art/Oral Language Activities

CLOTHESPIN PILGRIMS

Making the Dolls Remind students that Pilgrims come to America from all over the world–they are not only the settlers who came from England in 1620. Let students know that their Pilgrim dolls can be dressed differently, just like Molly's, depending on the places they come from.

You need:

wooden clothespins	pipe cleaners	scissors
fabric scraps (velvet, cotton, wool, lace)	ribbon	yarn
construction paper	paintbrushes	glue
colored waterproof markers	acrylic paints	

Steps:

1. Before students begin this activity, ask them to decide where their Pilgrim dolls come from. If you wish, assign different countries or have students make traditional Pilgrim dolls.

2. Using different colored markers, have students draw a face on one side of the "head" of a clothespin. For hair, let students paint the top and back of the head or glue on lengths of yarn. (Students may even wish to glue on a beard or mustache for Pilgrim men.)

3. For arms, show students how to wrap a pipe cleaner around each clothespin "neck."

4. Tell students that they can paint clothes on the rest of the clothespin, or they can make the clothes for a more elaborate doll.

- A cape can be made out of wool or velvet and slipped over the clothespin's head. Pull the pipe-cleaner arms through the cape's holes. Show students how to glue the inside of the cape to the clothespin.

- A collar can be made from a circle of lace or white construction paper. Show students how to glue the tabs closed around the neck of the clothespin.

- A skirt can be made from any fabric and wrapped under the pipe-cleaner arms and glued to the clothespin.

5. For finishing touches, suggest that students wrap ribbon shoes around the "feet" of the clothespins or a ribbon belt around the "waist." They can glue a circle of lace to the clothespin "head" for a lady's cap.

How to Use:

1. Have students pretend they are modern-day Pilgrims from different countries. Suggest that they interview family members or friends to learn about life abroad. Students can then use their Pilgrim dolls to report to the class and to explain why they have come to America.

2. Invite students to create a setting for their Pilgrims. It can be traditional or modern. Suggest that students color and cut out buildings, mountains, or trees, and that they include a tab that can be glued to the floor of the display for the figures to stand upright.

3. Have students use their clothespin Pilgrims to dramatize the scene from the book in which the children show Miss Stickley their Pilgrim dolls. Assign the roles of Molly, Elizabeth, Emma, Michael, Arthur, Hilda, and Miss Stickley. Invite students to make up their own dialogue for each character as they discuss the dolls and the meaning of Thanksgiving.

Cooperative Learning/Listening/Speaking

HERE'S TO MOLLY

There's More than One Way Remind students that in the story, Elizabeth expects the other children to behave in a certain way (for example, dress, speech, celebration of holidays). She does not understand that things can be done differently. Ask students what happens when Molly behaves differently. (Elizabeth gets everyone to make fun of Molly.) What does Miss Stickley teach the children? (There is more than one kind of Pilgrim.)

Ask students to share what they think are common ways of celebrating Thanksgiving. On the chalkboard make a chart showing foods students eat at Thanksgiving, guests they invite, places where they celebrate, and other traditions they associate with the holiday. As the chart is completed, discuss the results, focusing on entries that may be new ways of celebrating for some students. Help students discover that their preconceived ideas are not always correct and that people do celebrate in different ways.

Parents' Day Remind students that at the end of the book, Miss Stickley wants to meet Molly's mother. What might Miss Stickley say to Mama? What might Mama say to Miss Stickley? Have students pretend that it is Parents' Day at school. Suggest that some students take turns pretending to be Mama and Miss Stickley and dramatize what they might say to each other. Other students can pretend to be Molly's father and talk to Miss Stickley about the trials of factory work in New York City and what he now does at the store in Winter Hill.

Social Studies: Celebrating Sukkos Review with students that Molly's family celebrates the ancient harvest holiday of Sukkos. Explain that during this holiday Jewish families construct outdoor huts, called *sukkahs*, in which they eat their meals. The huts remind Jews of ancient times when people lived close to nature. The roof of a sukkah is made from branches and leaves. Fruits of the harvest, such as apples, grapes, corn, and peaches, are strung from the branches. During the holiday, people carry a long palm branch bound together with willow and myrtle branches in their right hands. They carry a fragrant fruit that looks like a big lumpy lemon, called *etrog*, in their left hands.

Make a miniature sukkah with your students. Turn a large carton on its side, cut off the top side, and have students replace the top with overhanging branches and leaves. Then divide the class into three groups and have each group make one of the decorations below for the sukkah.

- Let students create harvest chains to hang from the roof. On a threaded needle, knotted at the end, have students alternately string raw cranberries, peas, and corn kernels.

- Invite other students to hang long, brightly-colored ribbons from the roof and on the sides of the sukkah.

- Lastly, ask students to make holders for *etrogs* (or lemons) from plastic egg-shaped containers. Show students how to cover the containers with glue and dip them into a tin of mixed grains or dried vegetables. When dry, tell students to lay the etrogs on beds of colored tissue paper inside the containers. Then place the etrogs in the sukkah.

When completed, let small groups of students enjoy snack time or lunch in the sukkah. If weather permits, place the sukkah outdoors for more authenticity.

EXTENDED ACTIVITIES

Other Ways Explain that people all over the world celebrate harvest festivals like Thanksgiving, and each in a different way. Describe some of the harvest festivals listed below and invite the class to celebrate one or more of them.

• **Marten Gas** After a feast capped by an enormous cake made from hundreds of eggs, children in Sweden parade with hollowed-out squashes and pumpkins. Help your students hollow out vegetables to parade with. Cut the pumpkin or squash yourself, then let students take turns scooping out the insides with a large spoon. Have a large cake ready for the class to enjoy with their vegetables afterwards.

• **Mop Fair** In England at harvest time, the mayor of the town of Stratford-on-Avon wears a high hat and a coat with tails. He rings a bell to start the fair. At the fair there is a dancing bear and a merry-go-round. Your students can dramatize a trip to Mop Fair. Let one student be the mayor ringing the bell, and another the dancing bear. Other students can become a human "merry-go-round" and sing simple songs as they march around in a circle.

• **Kanto Matsuri** In Japan farmers celebrate the reaping of the rice harvest by wearing bright clothes and balancing long bamboo poles (*kantos*) strung with lanterns on their hands, hips, shoulders, or foreheads. Have costumed students try to balance yardsticks (or meter sticks) on their hands and shoulders. For an extra challenge, hang paper lanterns on the ends of the poles.

Sing-Songs Reread the chant on page 5 of the book that Elizabeth recites about Molly. Ask students why they think the children tease Molly so much. (She is different; she speaks with an accent; she dresses differently; she comes from a foreign place; she doesn't know about Thanksgiving.) At the end of the book, what does Molly learn about herself? (She can be proud of who she is; *all* Americans come from different backgrounds.) What does the whole class learn about Pilgrims? (There are many different kinds; they are still coming to America.)

Based upon her classmates' acceptance of Molly, have students create a new song that they might sing about her. For example:

My friend Molly,
You're awf'ly kind and sweet.
My friend Molly,
Your Pilgrim's awf'ly neat!

Then invite students to create songs that Molly might sing about other characters in the book, or teach them the ones below.

Tizzie Lizzie
You always like to tease,
Tizzie Lizzie,
You're oh so hard to please.

Dear Miss Stickley,
A teacher kind and true,
Dear Miss Stickley,
I'm happy thanks to you.

Social Studies: Ellis Island Explain to the class that some of the first Pilgrims to come to this country arrived in Plymouth, Massachusetts, in 1620, but between 1892 and 1943 Pilgrims, like Molly and her family, arrived through New York's Ellis Island. Encourage interested students to research the history of Ellis Island, now newly renovated as a historical site. Help students find pictures of real immigrants of this time to share with the class. Suggest that groups of students act out what it was like to arrive in America at that time and how the new Pilgrims might have felt when seeing the Statue of Liberty after their long ocean voyage.

PRE-READING ACTIVITIES

Meet the Author: Ezra Jack Keats

Born and raised in Brooklyn, New York, Keats (1916-1983) always yearned to be a painter, even though his ambition was only reluctantly encouraged by his parents and even though he had no formal art training. During the late 1930s, he became a mural artist on Works Progress Administration projects, helping to create the panoramic scenes of American history and American heroes that still adorn many post offices and other public buildings today. During World War II, Keats turned his skills to creating camouflage devices for the United States Air Corps. In 1948, he took a painting trip through Europe and returned to exhibit his works in New York City art galleries.

Keats went on to illustrate magazines, teach painting, and illustrate many children's books, among them Frances Carpenter's *Wonder Tales of Dogs and Cats*, Paul Showers's *In the Night*, and Patricia Martin's *The Rice Bowl Pet*. The first book he both wrote and illustrated was *The Snowy Day*, for which he won the 1963 Caldecott Medal. Keats's illustrative technique—combining collage with colorful drawings—has inspired many children's book artists.

Story Summary

In this version of the John Henry story, the author combines fact and legend to tell the story of this emancipated black man. As in the ballad, John Henry is born with a hammer in his hand, foreshadowing the way he will eventually earn his living. As a young man, he helps his father on the family farm, then moves away to work on a riverboat, where he saves the day by turning the huge paddle wheel after the driving rod breaks. Itching to use a hammer again, Henry goes to work on the railroad. He soon proves his mettle by saving his fellow workers from a cave-in.

By this time, Henry is already renowned for his strength. One day, a man brings an experimental steam drill to the tunnel site, claiming that it can do the work of six men. John Henry challenges him. Henry wins the race, but dies shortly thereafter from—as legend has it—exhaustion. (It is believed that in fact he probably died from a falling rock that crushed him.)

A Little Background

Before you read the book, tell students that the story is based on a true event and a real person. John Henry was one of thousands of emancipated slaves who, after the Civil War, helped build the transcontinental railroad. During the 1870s, Henry worked on the stretch of the Chesapeake and Ohio Railroad that was being laid across West Virginia, and he helped to build the Big Bend Tunnel. Using long-handled, ten-pound hammers, tunnel workers drove steel drills into the rocky mountainside to make holes that held dynamite. Explain that John Henry soon became a hero to his fellow workers, who admired his strength and courage and who felt threatened by machines that could take away their jobs. After John Henry's final courageous exploit, ballads were created to celebrate him. (The first written version appeared about 1900.) Legendary features were added to the ballad, such as John Henry being born "with a hammer in his hand" and John Henry dying from exhaustion after the race.

John Henry
Comprehension

How Does He Do It?

Finish each sentence to tell how John Henry does each deed.

1. He saves a riverboat by

_____

2. He helps lay tracks by

_____

3. He puts out a dynamite fuse by

_____

4. He wins a race by

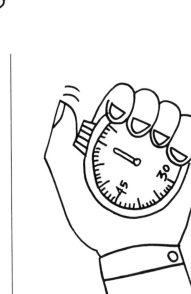

_____

• Choose one of John Henry's deeds. On the back of this page write a sentence telling how **you** might do the deed differently.

John Henry
Vocabulary: Onomatopoeia

What Do You Hear?

Write the word from the train that describes each sound below. Then write the circled letters in the numbered spaces in the sentence at the bottom. The sentence tells what John Henry is.

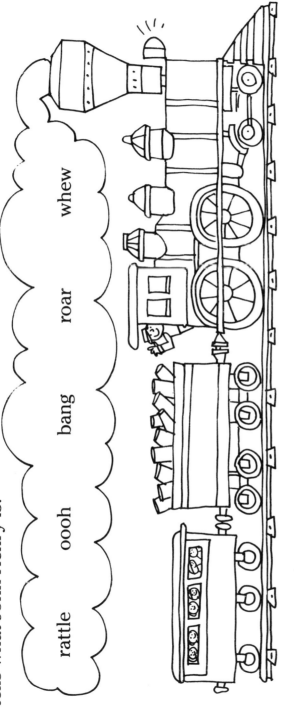

rattle   oooh   bang   roar   whew

1. The sound John Henry's hammer makes: ___ ___ ___ ⃝ ___
                                                    1

2. A sigh of relief: ___ ⃝ ___ ___
                        2

3. The sound a steam drill makes: ___ ___ ___ ⃝ ___
                                            3

4. The sound an engine makes: ___ ⃝ ___ ___
                                 4

5. A sound made by someone who is hurt: ___ ___ ⃝ ___
                                                5

John Henry is ___ ___ ___ ___ ___ .
             1   2   3   4   5

• Choose two words from the train. On the back of this page use each word in a sentence of your own that tells about John Henry.

John Henry
Story Structure: Character

Tunnel Talk

Name _____

What do you think John Henry's coworkers say while John Henry races the steam drill? Write what you think they say below.

- What do you think the man with the steam drill says during the race? Write your answer on the back of this page.

John Henry
Creative Writing

Rhyme and Rhythm

John Henry sings a poem as he hammers. On the lines below write a poem of your own about John Henry. An example has been done for you.

Bang goes the spike
into the hill.
John Henry works
with his friend Li'l Bill.

• Can you clap the rhythm of your poem? Circle the words in your poem that you would clap to.

JOHN HENRY'S COLLAGE

Picture Journeys Use this collage activity to help students develop an understanding of the different landforms and bodies of water John Henry experiences during his life.

You need:

John Henry silhouette pattern
several scraps and sheets of different kinds of paper
(colored construction paper, wallpaper, colored tissue paper,
butcher paper, stationery, wrapping paper, crepe paper)
oaktag   scissors   paste   marking pens

Steps:

1. Begin by reviewing the book illustrations. Ask students to find John Henry in the pictures and to describe his surroundings. Explain that Ezra Jack Keats created many of these landscapes by using torn and cut paper along with drawings. Encourage students to try tearing or cutting a craggy, high peak or a wavy river out of a piece of paper.

2. Reproduce the John Henry silhouette pattern for each student.

Then ask students to choose an incident in John Henry's life to illustrate in a collage. It could be one from the story or one that they think could have happened. Explain that they will paste the silhouette in a setting made from cut or torn paper.

3. Distribute the collage materials. Encourage students to experiment with different arrangements of their paper landscapes before pasting them and the silhouettes in place on oaktag. As a finishing touch, let students outline key features in their collages with marking pens.

4. Ask students to compose captions for their finished collages and then to share their work with the class. Display the collages and captions in sequence on a bulletin board or in a class big book.

Tracking the Tale Invite students to make a classroom railroad track that tells about important events in the story.

You need:

strips of colored construction paper   paste or glue
crayons and marking pens   hole punch   string

Steps:

1. Distribute five strips of paper to each student. Demonstrate how to glue the strips together to resemble train tracks.

2. Have each student make up a sentence about John Henry and copy it on the three railroad ties. Let students decorate each tie with symbols they feel represent John Henry, for example, hammers, riverboats, stars, and so on.

3. Connect all the tracks with yarn or staples, and display the entire length of your railroad along a classroom wall.

TRAIN TIME

A Train Book Explain that long ago Americans were excited and curious about the prospect of a transcontinental railroad, and they had many questions about it. Ask volunteers to suggest what these questions might have been, and list them on the chalkboard. For example: How fast can trains go? How are tracks built? How does a train engine get its power? What do trains carry? Who works on a train? Where is the train station nearest their neighborhoods? What different kinds of cars are on a train? In addition, have students research questions they might have about modern railroads. For example:

- Why would people choose to travel by plane instead of by train? (Provide airline and train schedules as a research aid.)
- What kinds of cargo are shipped by train today?
- What kinds of trains do commuters today depend upon? (commuter trains, subways)
- What are the train systems like in Europe and other countries?

Divide the class into groups of four or five to choose one question to investigate. Suggest that each group organize its findings into a *John Henry Train Book*. Have each group decide how to present information in both words and pictures. One or two group members can be responsible for putting the pages of the book in order while another illustrates a cover for the book. A fourth member can create a simple table of contents. Invite each group to show and read its book to the class. Put the finished books on a reading table for students to enjoy independently.

Books About Trains The following books are notable for vivid, information-filled pictures and diagrams.

- *Train Cargo* by June Behans, Children's Press, Chicago, 1974.
- *The Big Book of Real Trains* by Elizabeth Cameron, Grosset & Dunlap, New York, 1976.
- *Trains at Work* by Mary Elting, Harvey House, Irvington-On-Hudson, New York 1962.

A children's classic about the history of railroads is Maud and Miska Petersham's *The Story Book of Trains* (John C. Winston, 1947).

Maps and Media To enhance students' appreciation of the railway system, show a video tape of a real train ride. The "Ridin' the Rails" video series includes *National Geographic: Love Those Trains*, which documents trains from the past to the present, and *Cumbres and Toltec Scenic Railroad*, which features a narrow-gauge, steam locomotive trip through New Mexico to Colorado. (These and other train videos are available from Postings, P. O. Box 8001, Hilliard, Ohio 43026. Call 800-262-6604 for prices and ordering information.)

Before starting, point out the train's route on a U. S. map. Then after the video, invite students to tell about the parts they liked best, and discuss new or hard-to-understand information. Conclude the activity by asking students to write a letter to John Henry, describing their video train ride and thanking him for helping build the railroads that made their journey possible. Invite students to share their finished letters with the class.

EXTENDED ACTIVITIES

Remembering John Henry As a culminating activity, list the different story characters on the chalkboard and explain that each one has special memories of John Henry. For example, John Henry's mother remembers that her son was born with a hammer in his hand and crawled around the house banging it. Ask seven volunteers to each choose one character and to tell about John Henry as that person might, but without revealing the character's identity. Ask listeners to name the character who is speaking and to add any additional ideas about how that person might remember John Henry.

CAST OF
CHARACTERS
John Henry's mother
John Henry's father
the riverboat captain
Li'l Bill
the foreman on the railroad
the man trapped in the tunnel
the man with the steam drill

Conclude the activity by inviting students to tell why *they* will remember John Henry. Ask students to write and illustrate their responses, and display them on a bulletin board.

Social Studies: People and Machines Remind the class that steam engines were new in John Henry's time. Explain that John Henry and his fellow workers feared that new machines would eventually take their jobs away; John Henry won the race to prove that this was not true. Ask students to suggest tasks they think people can do better than machines. Conclude the activity by asking what else John Henry does that machines cannot do (sing a song, save his friends, help his parents). Then ask students what they can do that machines cannot (make up jokes, comfort a friend, work together on a class project).

Mapping the Story To summarize the story, use a large map of the United States to help students track John Henry's travels. Ask volunteers to locate the southeastern United States where John Henry was born and raised, the Mississippi River where he saved the riverboat, and West Virginia where he became a railroad worker. Point out the Atlantic and Pacific coasts, and explain that John Henry was helping to build a railroad that would unite them.

Ain't no hammers
Strike such fire,
Strike like lightning, Lawd,
And I won't tire!

Hammers like this, Lawd,
There's never been!
I'll keep swingin' 'em, Lawd,
Until we win!

Language Arts: Interviewing Suggest that students tell the story of John Henry to adults or older siblings at home or to a younger class. Storytellers can then ask the listeners for their reactions to John's race with the steam engine. Possible questions include:

- What do you think of John Henry?
- Why do you think he raced with a steam engine?
- How do you feel about the ending of the story?
- If you could, how would you change the ending?

Tell students to take notes during the interview, and invite them to share their responses with the class.

Drama: Actions and Rhythms Explain that the song John Henry sings in the book was sung later by railroad workers as they hammered spikes into the rails they were building. As they sang, they matched the rhythm of their actions with the song. Copy the lyrics on the chalkboard, and invite a small group of volunteers to practice reading and saying the words together. Call on another volunteer to look at the book illustrations, then pantomime John Henry's actions as he drives a spike with a heavy hammer. Ask the choral readers to say the poem in rhythm with the actor's movements. Extend the activity by inviting interested students to work in pairs to make up and act out rhymes whose rhythms match the tasks that other kinds of workers might do.

PRE-READING ACTIVITIES

Meet the Author: Paul Goble

Paul Goble was born on September 17, 1933, in Surrey, England. His parents made harpsichords. When he was a child, Goble's mother read to him books by Ernest Thompson Seton and Grey Owl, two writers he calls "true naturalists." Both authors wrote about American Indians and greatly influenced Goble's work, for "The world they wrote about was so different from the crowded island where I lived." Goble began acquiring a considerable library of books about Native Americans, and after finishing his courses at the Central School of Arts and Crafts in London, he made the first of many visits to the United States. He spent time on the reservations of the Sioux and Crow Indians in South Dakota and Montana. During these visits he was present at sacred dances, took part in ceremonies, and listened as his Indian friends spoke of their folklore and beliefs. His first book, *Red Hawk's Account of Custer's Last Battle*, was published in 1969. All his books have dealt with Indian life. *The Girl Who Loved Wild Horses*, the 1979 Caldecott winner, is a synthesis of many Native America tales. In it Goble expresses what he envisions as the Native American rapport with nature. He says, "Simply, the girl loves horses, and perhaps she becomes one." Goble now makes his home in the Black Hills of Deadwood, South Dakota.

Story Summary

An American Indian girl loves the horses that her people keep. She tends to them and spends as much time with them as she can. One day, she falls asleep among them. Suddenly a large thunderstorm comes up. Awakened by the storm, the girl jumps on the back of one of the terrorized horses. Instantly, she is swept away with the frightened herd as it gallops from the storm. When the herd finally stops, the girl knows that she and the horses are far away from her family. The following morning she is met by a handsome stallion, who tells her that he is the leader of the wild horses that live in the hills. He invites her to stay with them, and she happily accepts. A year goes by before some hunters from the girl's people spot her with the stallion and his herd leading a colt. The men return with other riders, and finally they capture the girl and return her to her family. But the girl is not happy, and her parents agree that she should return to the wild horses. Grateful, she returns home each year to bring her parents a colt. Then one year she doesn't come back. Some hunters report seeing a great stallion racing with a beautiful mare, and the people believe that the girl finally has become one of the wild horses.

Animal Transformations

Ask students to think about their favorite animals. Would they like to become that animal? As they call out answers, write students' responses on the chalkboard. Then tell them that the book they are about to read concerns a girl who loves horses. Do they think she will become a horse? Compare students' answers with the outcome of the story.

Wild and Tame

Discuss with the class the meaning of the words *wild* and *tame* as they apply to animals. Then write the words on the chalkboard, and ask students to name examples of animals that fit either category. List the animals under the appropriate headings as volunteers suggest them. Ask students under which heading they would put *horses*. Some students may be surprised that horses can go under both headings. Tell students to look for both kinds of horses as they read Paul Goble's book.

The Girl Who Loved Wild Horses
Comprehension

Name _____

Helping Hands

In the story the girl helps the horses. The horses help the people, too. Write each phrase from the blanket under the correct heading.

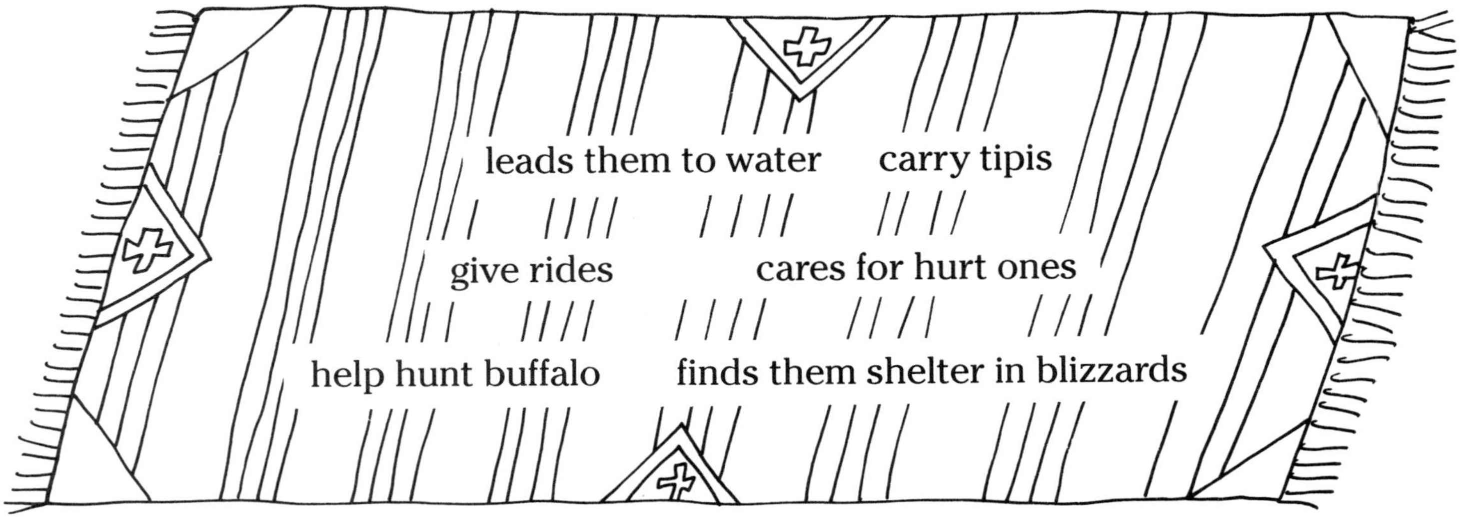

leads them to water

carry tipis

give rides

cares for hurt ones

help hunt buffalo

finds them shelter in blizzards

How the Girl Helps the Horses	How the Horses Help the People
1.	1.
2.	2.
3.	3.

• How does the stallion try to help the girl? Write your ideas on the back of this page.

The Girl Who Loved Wild Horses
Vocabulary

Name _____

Words for Wild Horses

Complete each sentence with a word about horses. The words you need are hidden in the puzzle.

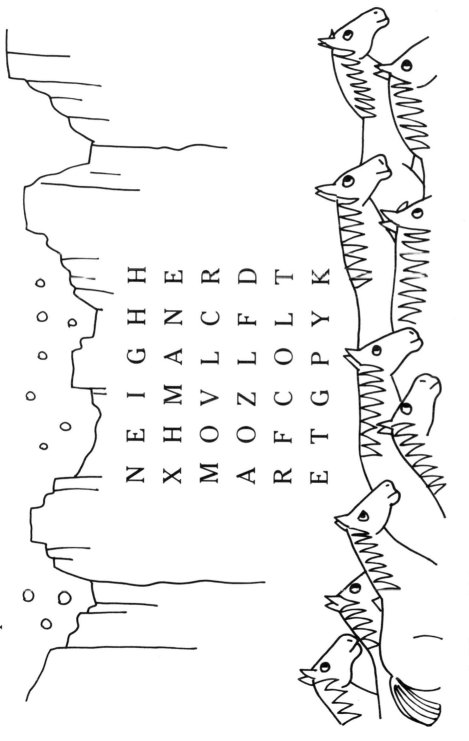

```
N   E   I   G   H   H
X   H   M   A   N   E
M   O   V   L   C   R
A   O   Z   L   F   D
R   F   C   O   L   T
E   T   G   P   Y   K
```

1. The wild horses live together in a _____.

2. When horses make sounds, they _____.

3. A young horse is a _____.

4. The _____ grows along a horse's neck.

5. A female horse is a _____.

6. When horses run, they _____.

● Find a word in the puzzle for a horse's foot.

The Girl Who Loved Wild Horses
Story Structure: Character

Name _____

Head of the Herd

The girl in the story loves the stallion. Choose the words from the box that describe the stallion. Write the words on the waterfall.

free	strong	afraid	proud	handsome
	sickly	fast	mighty	lost	brave

• On the back of this page write a sentence to tell why you think the stallion likes the girl.

The Girl Who Loved Wild Horses
Creative Writing

Name _____

Sensing a Storm

The storm changes the girl's life. Write a complete sentence about the storm in the story or a storm you have seen using each phrase below.

1. the scent of rain _____

_____

2. a fresh breeze _____

_____

3. a flash of lightning _____

_____

4. distant thunder _____

_____

5. angry clouds _____

_____

6. the crash and rumbling _____

_____

• On the back of this page try using your sentences and ideas to write a poem about a storm.

The Girl Who Loved Wild Horses
Creative Writing

Name _____

A Horse Is a Horse

At the end of the story, the girl's family believes she has become a horse. What do **you** think? Write your ideas about what has become of the girl who loved wild horses. Explain your ideas, too.

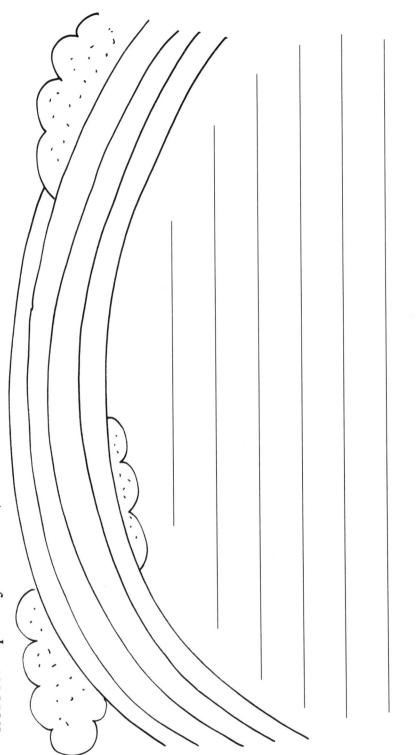

• On the back of this page write something that you would ask the girl if you met her.

Art Activities

BEAUTIFUL BLANKETS

A Blanket to Dye For Remind students that the girl in the story has a beautiful blanket. Explain that many Native American groups are famous for their handwoven blankets. Traditionally, these weavers create their own thread from wool and dye it as well. Invite students to try dyeing fabric themselves to make into small blankets for dolls or stuffed animals or as place mats.

You need:

white cotton rectangles, 9" x 12"   pie tins   newspaper
berries (raspberries, blueberries, or strawberries)
onion skins   tea bags   saffron   water

Steps:

1. Spread newspaper over four or five worktables. Provide each table with one of the following materials for making dye: onion skins, berries, tea bags, or saffron.

2. Assign each student to a table. Explain that each table will make a different dye. Have students place the dye materials in pie tins of warm water. Students who are working with berries will need to crush them first. (Diluted grape juice can be substituted for the berries.)

3. Help students decide when their dyes are dark enough. Then provide each table with pieces of cotton fabric for each student. Show students how to color the cloth by dipping it into the dye.

4. Hang the cloth squares to dry with clothespins on a string stretched across the back of the room, placing newspaper on the floor to catch the drips. Later, provide permanent markers, cloth scraps, and other materials for decorating the dyed cloths. Display the final products on a bulletin board for others to see.

Tipi Tapestries Ask students to look through *The Girl Who Loved Wild Horses* to note some of the bold patterns Paul Goble paints on the tipis, horses, and clothing. Then invite students to make pattern pictures of their own for tipi designs.

You need:

colored construction paper   scissors   glue
small circles, squares, triangles, rectangles, and other shapes
cut from construction paper

Steps:

1. Ask students to choose a large piece of colored construction paper to use as a background.

2. Show students how to work with the small colored cutout shapes to develop repeating patterns on their papers. Remind students to consider both color and shape as they make their decisions. Encourage them to cut their own shapes from paper, too. When students are satisfied with their patterns, tell them to glue the pieces in place.

3. Display the finished pattern pictures in tipi outlines on mural paper or on a bulletin titled "PLAINS" TIPIS.

Art/Oral Language Activities

LET'S HEAR IT FOR HORSES

To develop students' appreciation of horses, have them create these artistic ones.

Horse Puppets After students make these puppet heads, invite them to retell Paul Goble's story from the point of view of one of the horses.

You need:

plastic foam cups		colored construction paper	
scissors	colored markers	glue	yarn

Steps:

1. Provide each student with a plastic foam cup. Help students make a hole in the side of the cup large enough to stick a finger through.

2. Next have students cut out ears from construction paper and show them where to glue the ears to the cup (the finger hole should be at the bottom).

3. Let students draw eyes, nostrils, and a mouth on the cup as shown.

4. Finally, show students how to make a mane. Loop a piece of yarn around your fingers as shown. Slip the yarn off your fingers, then tie yarn between the loops. Cut the ends. Glue the yarn onto the cup with the fringe between the horse's ears.

5. To use their puppets, tell students to stick their index fingers in the hole and then let the horses speak for themselves. Set aside time for the puppets to perform.

Stallion Statues These simple stand-up horses are easy to make and can be used as toys, for table decorations, or as puppets to act out the story.

You need:

plastic foam trays	scissors	colored markers	pencils

Steps:

1. Ask students to bring from home two clean plastic foam meat or vegetable trays.

2. Show students how to sketch the body of a horse on one tray with a pencil. On the second tray show students how to draw two sets of legs as shown.

3. Let students color their horses with markers.

4. Have students cut out the body and legs. Then demonstrate how to set the body into the slits at the top of the legs to make the horse stand. As an alternative, students can also use wooden spring clothespins for their horses' legs or oaktag or cardboard for their bodies.

More Horses Set up a reading corner in your classroom devoted to horses, enhanced by posters or pictures cut from magazines. In addition to *The Girl Who Loved Wild Horses* you might display the following titles:

- *Fritz and the Beautiful Horses* by Jan Brett
- *Flip and the Morning* by Wesley Dennis
- *Wild Horses of the Red Desert* by Glen Rounds
- *Song of the Horse* by Marcia Sewall

Invite horse fans to contribute other materials to the display. Encourage students to tell the class about other books they have read on the subject.

Cooperative Learning/Listening /Speaking

LET'S LASSO

These lively games will help work off excess energy. Play them on a playground or in the gym.

Capture the Horse Remind students that the hunters were not able to capture the mighty stallion with their ropes. Then challenge the class to see who can rope a "horse." Make several lassos from clothesline and set up some chairs or trash baskets as horses. Let students practice tossing the lassos. Then divide the class into three or four teams. Have each team line up about three yards from a "horse." Draw a line in the dirt or on the floor in front of the first person on each team. Tell students that they will have a lasso relay race. Each teammate gets two chances to lasso the "horse," starting with the first player. As soon as one player has tried to lasso twice, the next player gets two chances. The object is to see which team can capture the most horses the fastest. As students become more proficient at the game, challenge them to stand farther back from the horses and to invent variations on how to play the game.

Horsing Around This is a version of the game "Red Light, Green Light" for groups of 8 to 10 students to play. Before starting, have students work out a specific horse step for each of these terms: walk, trot, gallop, canter, buck. Then choose one player to be "It." The rest of the players are horses. "It" stands on one side of the playground, and the horses on the other. "It" turns his or her back to the horses, calls out one horse's name, and gives directions for how many and what kind of step that horse can take. For example, "It" might say, "Amy, take three trotting steps." While Amy is taking three trotting steps toward "It," "It" counts to 10 as slowly or quickly as he or she wants with back turned to the horses. During this time the other horses try to move up too. However, when "It" reaches 10, he or she turns quickly around and tries to catch any of the horses (except Amy) who are still moving. If any horses are caught, they must go back to the starting line. Play resumes as "It" gives directions to another horse and continues until one horse is close enough to tag "It." That player then becomes "It," and the game starts again. Repeat as time and interest allow.

Body Language Remind students that the stallion was mighty and proud. Then ask volunteers to express these attributes using only body language. Ask guiding questions, such as: How does someone who is mighty and proud stand? Walk? Run? Then invite everyone to pantomime these actions of the various characters in the story:

- The stallion is being hunted. How does he fight?
- The girl is captured. How does she feel?
- The storm is fierce. How do the horses act?
- The parents are happy to see their daughter again. How do they show it?

EXTENDED ACTIVITIES

The Story Line As a summarizing activity, write the following events on the chalkboard out of order or on strips of paper, and ask volunteers to number the sentences so they are in the correct sequence.

1. The girl falls asleep on a hot day.
2. A storm comes up.
3. The horses gallop away in fear.
4. The girl and the horses are far away.
5. The girl meets the stallion.
6. The hunters capture the girl.
7. The girl's parents let her return to the stallion.
8. The girl gives a colt to her parents.
9. The girl is never seen again.
10. The hunters see a mare with the wild stallion.

Reading: More by Goble If students enjoyed *The Girl Who Loved Wild Horses*, they may want to read some of Paul Goble's other Native American tales. Suggest they check the school or local public library for these Goble titles: *Buffalo Woman*, *The Gift of the Sacred Dog*, *Star Boy*, *The Great Race*, and *Iktomi and the Boulder*.

Social Studies: Real Wild Horses

Your students may be interested to learn that there are about 50,000 wild horses in the western states, particularly in Nevada. A 1971 Congressional act protects these animals as "living symbols of the historic and pioneer spirit of the West." However, in recent years this protection has been so successful that the land on which the horses roam can no longer sustain such large herds. As a result, the fate of the wild horses is in jeopardy. The federal Bureau of Land Management (BLM) runs an adoption program for the horses. Students interested in learning more about the program might write to the bureau at 1849 C Street NW, Room 5600, Washington, D. C. 20240.

Social Studies: Comparing Cultures The people described in Paul Goble's book are primarily those living on the plains of the midwestern United States. Invite interested students to read further to learn about other Native American groups in order to compare their way of life with what they know about the Plains Indians. An excellent place to start their research is with the book *First Came the Indians* by anthropologist M. J. Wheeler, Atheneum, 1983.

Social Studies: What About the Buffalo? Remind students that the girl's people hunt buffalo. Explain that these animals were very important to Indians of the plains. Ask interested volunteers to find out more about the buffalo, including answers to these questions:

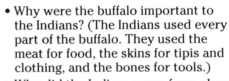

- Why were the buffalo important to the Indians? (The Indians used every part of the buffalo. They used the meat for food, the skins for tipis and clothing, and the bones for tools.)
- Why did the Indians move from place to place? (They followed the buffalo herds across the plains.)
- What happened to the buffalo? (White hunters killed too many of them, and the herds began to shrink.)

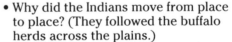

Invite students to share other information they find of interest, as well as pictures of wild herds found in Yellowstone National Park today. As a follow-up, read aloud Carl Sandburg's poem, "Buffalo Dusk." Encourage students to share their reactions to the poem.

PRE-READING ACTIVITIES

Meet the Author: Jean Fritz Born on November 16, 1915, Jean Fritz spent her first 13 years in Hankow, China, where her American parents lived and worked. An only child, she spent much time reading books about faraway places, especially the United States. She longed to go there to do such "American things" as celebrating Thanksgiving and the Fourth of July. After graduating from Wheaton College and starting her own family, Fritz indulged her love of America and Americans by writing history and historical fiction for children. One of her first books, *The Cabin Faced West* (1958), was based on the life of Fritz's great-great-grandmother, an early pioneer in Pennsylvania. Although she has written other types of books, notably *The Animals of Dr. Schweitzer* (1958), Fritz's main focus continues to be on American roots, particularly the Revolutionary period. Her books about that era, such as *George Washington's Breakfast* (1969), are known for their precise historical details and their good humor. *And Then What Happened, Paul Revere?* was named in 1973 as an Outstanding Book of the Year by the *New York Times* and as a Best Book by the *School Library Journal*. Fritz has also written articles for *Horn Book*, *The New Yorker, Atlantic*, and other magazines.

Meet the Artist: Trina Schart Hyman Hyman was born on April 8, 1939, in Philadelphia, Pennsylvania, and grew up in nearby farm country. From the age of six on, she was determined to be an illustrator, and after graduating from high school, she studied at the Philadelphia Museum School of Art. Among her many illustrated works are *Greedy Mariani* by Dorothy Carter and *Magic in the Mist* by Margaret Kimmel, which were 1975 and 1976 entries in the Children's Book Council's Children's Book Showcase. In addition to her illustration work, Hyman has also served as art director for *Cricket* magazine. She lives on a farm in New Hampshire.

Story Summary Sam Adams is different. He doesn't wear fancy clothes like his friends; he is brave enough to speak out against the King of England, who rules the American colonies; and he refuses to learn how to ride a horse. While important people ride on horses, Sam Adams walks about the streets of Boston with his dog, planting thoughts about independence and planning and encouraging acts of rebellion against the British government and troops, such as the famous Boston Tea Party. When he serves as the Massachusetts representative to the First Continental Congress in Philadelphia in 1774, Sam reluctantly wears proper clothes. But he still refuses to ride a horse. By April of 1775, Adams is considered a traitor by the King for his views on American independence. With a price on his head, he flees the Redcoats when warned by Paul Revere. Finally, John Adams convinces his cousin that an American statesman could only do the new American nation proud if he would ride on a horse. After a painful riding lesson, Sam enters Philadelphia on horseback in October of 1775 to attend the Second Continental Congress, ready for his place in history.

Seeing the Past After reading every three or four pages, point to the illustrations and ask students to pick out details that show what colonial cities such as Boston were like 200 years ago. Discuss with students the richly detailed pictures that show cobblestone streets, British flags, shop signs of the times (using *Ye* instead of *The*), sailing ships, and colonial clothes, tools, furnishings, conveyances, and buildings. Encourage volunteers to compare the cities of Sam Adams's day with modern cities.

What Are You Like, Sam Adams?

Pretend you are Sam Adams. Fill in the blanks on the form to tell about Sam.

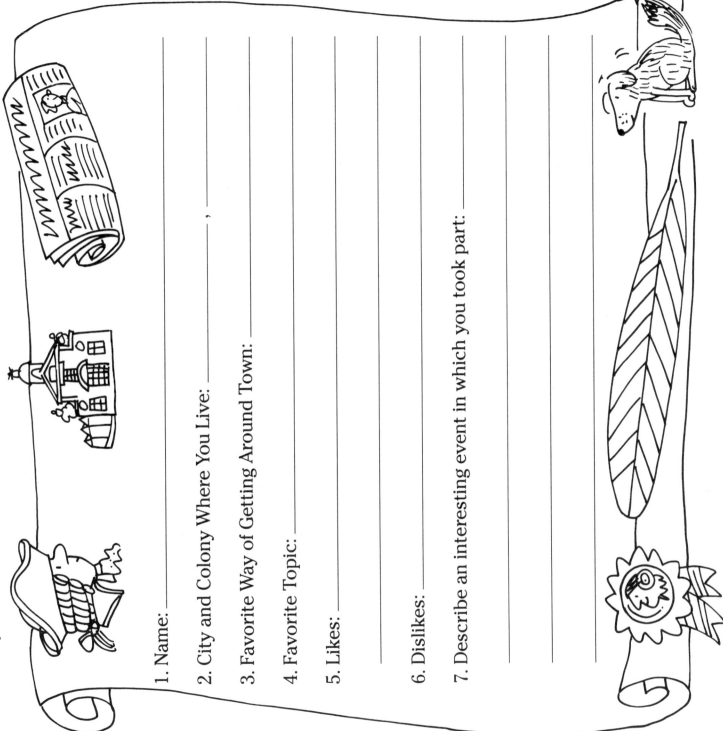

1. Name: ——————————————————————

2. City and Colony Where You Live: ——————————, ——————

3. Favorite Way of Getting Around Town: ——————————————

4. Favorite Topic: ————————————————————————

5. Likes: ————————————————————————————

6. Dislikes: ——————————————————————————

7. Describe an interesting event in which you took part: ——————

• On the back of this page write the name of a job you think Sam Adams should have.

Why Don't You Get a Horse, Sam Adams?
Vocabulary: Figurative Language

Name _____

In Other Words

Write the phrase from the box that means the same thing as the words below each line.

| drop in at | fly for his life | brains behind |
| hold his tongue | eyes | sit still under his wig |

1. Sam Adams and his dog _____ shops and taverns.

visit

2. Sam simply will not _____ about independence.

stop talking

3. When his cousin wants him to ride a horse, Sam just _____ it suspiciously.

looks at

4. At the first meeting in Philadelphia, Sam tries hard to _____ .

keep his ideas to himself

5. When the Redcoats come looking for him, Sam feels it his duty to _____ .

get away safely

6. Sam and John Hancock are the _____ the Revolution.

leaders of

- On the back of this page write about a time when **you** had to hold your tongue and sit still under your wig.

Why Don't You Get a Horse, Sam Adams?
Story Structure: Sequence

Revolutionary Talk

People have a lot to talk about where Sam Adams lives. Read the sentences in the box. Then write them in the speech bubbles in the order in which they happen.

Sam Adams is in Philadelphia, and I hear he rode on a horse!
A band of men just dumped a load of tea into the harbor!
England is making us pay a tax on everything that's printed!
The Redcoats are coming, and Paul Revere's spreading the alarm!

1.

2.

3.

4.

• If you lived during colonial times, what would you talk about? Write your ideas on the back of this page.

Why Don't You Get a Horse, Sam Adams?
Story Structure: Setting

America Then and Now

Tell or show how things have changed since Sam Adams's time by drawing pictures or writing words to complete the chart.

	In Sam Adams's Day	Now
Houses and Other Buildings		
Clothes		
Transportation		
Communication (How Ideas Get Around)		

• Suppose you could go back in time to visit colonial Boston. On the back of this page write a few sentences telling what you would like to do there.

Why Don't You Get A Horse, Sam Adams?
Creative Writing

A Dog's Tale

Suppose Sam Adams's dog Queue could talk and write. What would he say about Sam? Pretend you are Queue. Write a letter to a dog-friend to tell what spending a day with Sam is like.

Name _____

Dear _____,

_____, 17 ____

(Date)

_____
_____
_____
_____
_____
_____
_____
_____

Your friend,

_____

- On the back of this page draw a picture of Queue and Sam to send to Queue's friend.

PATCHES AND PATRIOTS

Patchwork Designs Invite students to design and draw pictures or symbols that represent key events or ideas in the book. Then combine the finished pictures to create a patchwork story-quilt to display.

You need:

6" x 6" oaktag squares	scratch paper	pencils	crayons
colored markers	staples or masking tape		

Steps:

1. Introduce the activity by displaying an old patchwork quilt or showing pictures of antique ones from a book. Ask students to brainstorm for a list of events, people, things, and ideas from the book that could be shown in patchwork squares. Write the list on the chalkboard.

2. Distribute art materials. Explain that each student will make a square for a class quilt about Sam Adams and his life in Boston. Then ask students to choose an idea from the list. Encourage them to use scratch paper to work out their designs before finalizing them on the oaktag squares. Ask students to sign their names in the lower right-hand corner of their squares.

> Queue   a sailing ship
> Sam Adams in his
>   scruffy clothes
> a Redcoat   a horse
> an old house in Boston
> the Boston Tea Party
> Sam's wig   a sword
> Paul Revere on his horse
> a horse-drawn carriage
> a statue of Sam   a flag

3. Tape or staple the squares together to replicate a patchwork quilt, and display the finished product on a classroom wall. Invite each student to tell the class what his or her square shows.

As a culminating activity, take pictures of the quilt or have students copy it. Invite them to take the photos or illustrations home to tell the story of Sam Adams to their families.

A Sculpture Show Use this activity to help students focus on American heroes.

You need:

modeling clay	tempera paints		paintbrushes
newspapers	pens	pencils	index cards

Steps:

1. Introduce the activity by asking students to review the pictures on pages 38 and 39 of the book that show statues of American heroes in the Revolutionary period. Discuss why all of these heroes (except Sam) are shown on horseback. (This was the way warriors and patriots traveled and fought in those days.) Invite students to tell about other heroes of the past and present that they could portray in a statue. For example: an astronaut, Martin Luther King, or any "unsung" local hero. List students' ideas on the chalkboard.

2. Cover work tables with newspaper, and distribute the modeling clay. Give students time to work with the clay to create small busts or statues of their heroes. After the statues have dried, let students paint them.

3. Invite students to write labels on index cards that tell who the person is and what he or she did for America. Display the sculptures and labels on windowsills or shelves. Encourage students to visit the "sculpture gallery" in their free time and to ask family members or other classes to enjoy the exhibit, too.

WORD POWER

Poster Protests To impress upon students the power of the written word, invite them to work in groups of three or four to make posters or buttons that present Sam Adams's ideas.

You need:

| poster paper | pencils | scratch paper | crayons and markers |

Steps:

1. Discuss with students the various things that made Sam Adams angry: being ruled by a country across the ocean (England); being taxed for day-to-day goods and activities; having soldiers take over the town; being hunted down by soldiers when he spoke his mind. Then discuss the methods of protest and persuasion that were available at that time: speaking in person to others or writing things that could be distributed by hand or posted (newspapers, pamphlets, posters, and so on). Invite volunteers to tell about messages they see on contemporary buttons, posters, or bumper stickers, for example, "I Brake for Wildlife" or "Get Out and Vote."

2. Distribute art materials. Invite each group to think of a slogan or message that states one of Sam Adams's big ideas. Suggest that one group member use scratch paper to plan how the message should be placed on the button or poster. Members can work together to plan and execute the accompanying pictures or designs. A third member might copy the message in its final form.

3. Ask the groups to show their posters and buttons to the class. Then alternate daily displaying each button or poster under the heading SAM ADAMS'S MESSAGE FOR TODAY. Groups may wish to make copies of their buttons for classmates to wear on that day. Buttons can be fastened with doublestick masking tape or safety pins.

On-the-Spot Newscasts Discuss with the class recent TV news broadcasts they have seen in which reporters at the scene of an event report on what is happening and interview witnesses and passers-by. Ask students to list exciting events in the story, for example the burning of the tax office, the arrival of the British soldiers on the Boston Common, the Boston Tea Party, and Paul Revere's ride. Invite students to work in groups of four or five to choose an event and to enact an on-the-spot TV coverage of it. One member can be the TV anchorperson in the studio, and another the on-the-spot reporter. Other group members can play the parts of the key figures, such as Sam Adams or Paul Revere, and of ordinary citizens being interviewed. After a brief rehearsal, let each group present its live news story to the class.

Words in Context Ask students to listen carefully as you read sentences from the book that contain new vocabulary words. Write the new words on the chalkboard, and ask students to choose the correct meanings from two possibilities you present orally. For example:

- His clothes were *shabby* and plain.
  (Does *shabby* mean "fancy" or "old and worn-out"?)
- His house was in *disrepair*.
  ("bad shape" or "good condition"?)
- Sam did his *fiercest* talking when the Redcoats fired.
  ("happiest" or "angriest"?)
- Two servants *boosted* Sam onto the horse.
  ("lifted" or "threw"?)

Ask students to tell how they arrived at the correct meaning, and encourage them to use the new words in sentences of their own.

IDEAS TO KEEP

Geography: The 13 Colonies Culminate the story by displaying a large wall map of the United States. Point out the Atlantic coast, and invite volunteers to identify the 13 states that made up the original British colonies (New Hampshire, Massachusetts, Rhode Island, Connecticut, New York, New Jersey, Pennsylvania, Delaware, Maryland, Virginia, North Carolina, South Carolina, and Georgia). Ask a volunteer to find the colony where Sam and John Adams lived (Massachusetts) and Pennsylvania, the colony to which the cousins traveled. Challenge the class to use the mileage scale to find the distance between Boston and Philadelphia. How far did Sam Adams have to travel? Now ask them over how many miles the 13 colonies stretched. Have students speculate how long it would have taken Sam Adams to travel the length of the 13 colonies by horse, by horse and carriage, and by modern transportation.

Music: Colonial Tunes Discuss patriotic songs that students know, such as "The Star-Spangled Banner" and "America the Beautiful." Explain that colonial Americans also sang songs that reflected their ideas about freedom and courage. Play some of the songs that inspired Americans of Sam Adams's time. By writing to *Colonial Williamsburg*, Box C, Williamsburg, Virginia 23185, you can obtain information about and prices for such records as "Fifes and Drums," "Jefferson's Music," and "Songs of Liberty–Revolutionary War." Encourage students to learn and sing the songs or to play the recordings as background music for their "sculpture gallery" (see page 53). Invite interested students to play along with the songs with rhythm and wind instruments.

Ideas in Flags Show the class the British flag that appears on pages 7, 16, 25, and 26. Explain that the symbols and colors in any flag stand for ideas important to the people who fly it. Point out that in the flag of the United States, the 13 stripes stand for the thirteen original colonies. Red stands for courage, white stands for purity, and blue stands for justice. Ask the class what they think the 50 stars stand for (the 50 states). Explain that as new states become part of the country, the number of stars on the flag changes. Invite interested students to find pictures in encyclopedias or almanacs of their state flag, the flags of the original 13 colonies, or the flag of another nation they are interested in. Encourage students to make copies of the flags and to display them with labels that give the name of the flag and tell what the colors and symbols stand for.

In addition, suggest that students design a flag for their classroom, school, or community, then show their designs to classmates and explain what the colors and symbols stand for.

Thinking Skills: Predicting
Ask students to imagine that Sam Adams could visit their community today. What things or situations do they think might surprise him most? Students can work in pairs to develop and present skits in which a guide shows Sam Adams a "modern" situation, and Sam asks questions about it for the guide to answer.

EXTENDED ACTIVITIES

independence
revolution
republic
statesman
governor
taxes
representative
traitor
nation
declaration
colony

Vocabulary: Social Studies Words On the chalkboard list these words from the story. Invite volunteers to each choose one word and to find its meaning in a dictionary. Ask students to copy the word and its definition, then to use it in a sentence about Sam Adams. Ask students to read their sentences to the class. You might compile the definitions into a "Sam Adams Colonial Dictionary" to display in your writing center. Invite students to add more pages to it as they discover more colonial-related words through independent reading or research.

Social Studies: You Have a Right! Discuss some of the English actions Sam Adams and other colonists objected to. Emphasized in the book are the British attempts to keep people like Sam from speaking freely, the quartering of troops on private land, the questioning of private citizens as they went about their daily lives, and the bursting into and searching of private homes.

we have the right...

Explain that Sam and other representatives made sure that the new Constitution would guarantee Americans freedom from these sorts of intrusions. These freedoms (10 in all) are listed in the Constitution's Bill of Rights, adopted on December 15, 1791. For students to better appreciate what the founding fathers of our country accomplished, divide the class into cooperative learning groups to create their own bill of rights for the classroom. If available, pass out copies of the real Bill of Rights for students to refer to. Suggest that groups discuss 10 rights or freedoms they feel should be allowed in the classroom or school. Tell group members to write and illustrate their own bill of rights to present to the class. Then, with the class, discuss each group's proposed bill of rights for responsibility and practicability. If feasible, combine the groups' bills of rights into a class guide.

Math: Travels with Sam Remind the class that in Sam Adams's day, there were no cars, trains, or planes. His means of transportation included walking, horses, and stagecoaches. Write the following problems on the chalkboard for students to solve.

• Sam plans to walk from one Massachusetts town to the next. It takes him 1 hour to walk 3 miles. How many hours will it take him to walk 9 miles? (3 hours) If he stops to rest for 2 hours, how long will his trip be? (5 hours)

• If Sam Adams gets on a horse, he can ride 11 miles in 1 hour. How many miles can he ride in 3 hours? (33 miles) How many more miles can he go in 3 hours on a horse than he can walking? (24 more miles)

• A stagecoach travels 10 miles an hour. If Sam rides in a stagecoach, how long will it take him to travel 50 miles? (5 hours) If the stagecoach stops for 1 hour, how long will the trip be? (6 hours)

Follow up by asking students which method of travel is the fastest for Sam Adams. Which do they think would be the most comfortable? What are some of the pros and cons of each means of travel? Conclude by reminding students how much faster people can travel today than they could in the 1770s.

SHOOTING STARS

Use this bulletin board to discuss the theme and introduce the books in this unit.

You need:

red, white, yellow, and blue construction paper
glue   scissors   cannon pattern (page 58)
child pattern (page 59)   star pattern (page 59)
book clues (page 60)
colored markers   stapler or thumbtacks

Steps:

1. Cover the bulletin board with red construction paper. Write SHOOTING STARS and AMERICA AND THE AMERICANS as shown in black marker or in white and yellow cutout letters.

2. Reproduce and cut out the patterns on pages 58 and 59. Trace the cannon pattern onto blue construction paper and cut out. Attach the cannon to the lower left side of the bulletin board.

3. Color in the child cutout and place above the cannon.

4. Trace the star pattern six times onto yellow construction paper and cut out the yellow stars. Place the stars on the bulletin board as shown. Draw lines coming from the stars.

5. Cut out six strips from white construction paper, and write a book title on each one. Attach each book title beside a star.

How to Use:

Cut out the six book clues, and ask six volunteers to each color one. Ask another volunteer to read the book titles on the bulletin board to the class. Then ask the students with the book clues to figure out which book titles their clues go with and to paste the book clue in the center of the appropriate star. Discuss the title of the unit, AMERICA AND THE AMERICANS, and ask students to predict what each book might be about.

CANNON PATTERN

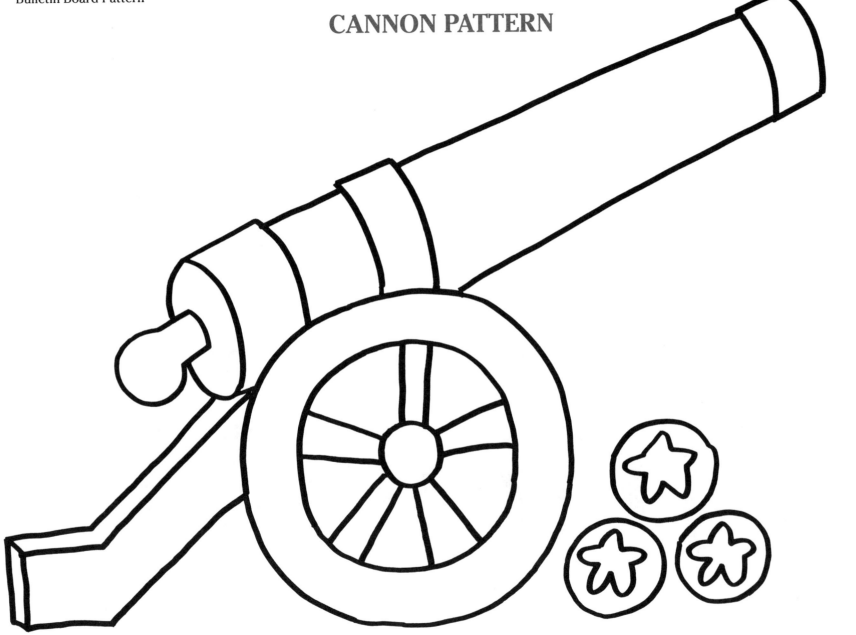

CHILD PATTERN AND STAR PATTERN

BOOK CLUES

The Erie Canal

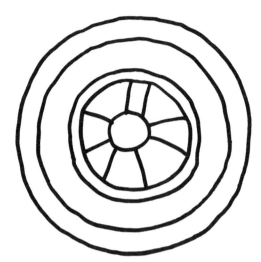

Wagon Wheels

Molly's Pilgrim

John Henry

The Girl Who Loved
Wild Horses

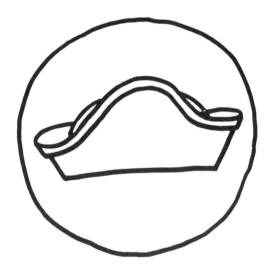

Why Don't You Get
a Horse, Sam Adams?

America and the Americans
Word Game

American Words

Here's a word game you can play. See how many words you can make with the letters in this word:

AMERICANS

The first one is done for you:

1. *American*

2. _____

3. _____

4. _____

5. _____

6. _____

7. _____

8. _____

9. _____

10. _____

11. _____

12. _____

13. _____

14. _____

15. _____

16. _____

17. _____

18. _____

19. _____

20. _____

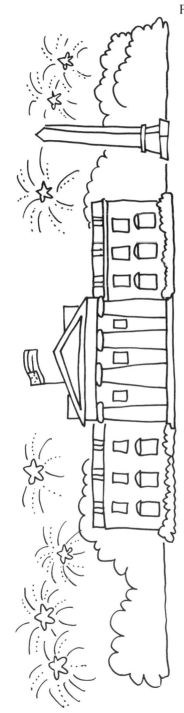

• Check to see that you spelled all your words correctly.

America and the Americans
Creative Writing

Name the State

In the story *Wagon Wheels* the Muldie family moves to Kansas. Here is a riddle one of the boys might have written about his new state.

My state is about in the middle of the United States. Its capital is Topeka. One of its most famous towns is Dodge City. That's because many famous cowboys have lived here.

Now write a riddle about your state or a state you know about. Give at least three facts.

• On the back of this page draw a picture to go with your riddle.

ANSWERS TO STUDENT WORKSHEETS

THE ERIE CANAL

Page 6: 1. The song is about the Erie Canal. 2. Sal is a mule. 3. Sal pulls the barge. 4. The barge carries people and cargo. 5. Sal travels 15 miles. • Everyone gets down.

Page 7: 1. hay 2. canal 3. pal 4. Buffalo 5. lock 6. down

Page 8: 1. to 4. Check to be sure students follow directions correctly. 5. Hudson River • New York

Page 9: Students' interviews with Sal will vary.

WAGON WHEELS

Page 14: Students' answers will vary. Possible: Chapter I–The Muldies build a prairie dugout. Chapter II–The Osage give the people of Nicodemus food and firewood. Chapter III–Mr. Muldie leaves to look for better land. Chapter IV–The Muldie boys follow their father to their new home in Solomon City.

Page 15: 1. dugout 2. cornmeal 3. firewood 4. saddlebags 5. rattlesnake • post rider

Page 16: 1. The boys and their father arrive in Nicodemus. 2. The family builds a dugout 3. Ed Muldie leaves to find land with trees and hills. 4. The boys get a letter from their father. 5. The boys leave Nicodemus to join their father. 6. The boys find their father.

Page 17: Students' diary entries will vary.

MOLLY'S PILGRIM

Page 22: 1. false 2. true 3. true 4. false 5. true 6. false

Page 23: 1. Yiddish 2. Russia 3. synagogue 4. Sukkos 5. Jewish 6. tenement • Goraduk

Page 24: Russia–She cannot go to school; She is afraid of the Cossacks. New York City–She lives in a tenement; Her father works in a factory. Winter Hill–She lives in a nice apartment; She speaks differently from the other children. • New York City and Winter Hill

Page 25: Students' stories will vary.

JOHN HENRY

Page 30: 1. turning the wheel 2. hammering spikes 3. hitting it with his hammer 4. working faster than a steam engine

Page 31: 1. bang 2. whew 3. rattle 4. roar 5. oooh; a hero

Page 32: Students' tunnel talk will vary.

Page 33: Students' poems will vary.

THE GIRL WHO LOVED WILD HORSES

Page 38: How the Girl Helps the Horses–leads them to water, cares for hurt ones, finds them shelter in blizzards; How the Horses Help the People–give rides, help hunt buffalo, carry tipis

Page 39: 1. herd 2. neigh 3. colt 4. mane 5. mare 6. gallop • hoof

Page 40: free, strong, proud, handsome, fast, mighty, brave

Page 41: Students' storm sentences will vary.

Page 42: Students' ideas will vary.

WHY DON'T YOU GET A HORSE, SAM ADAMS?

Page 48: 1. Samuel Adams 2. Boston, Massachusetts 3. walking 4. American independence 5. Possible: talking with other citizens, America, Queue, cousin John; 6. Possible: Redcoats, the King of England, tea taxes, riding horseback, fancy clothes and wigs; 7. Possible: I planned the "tea party" in Boston Harbor. I went to the Constitutional Convention and helped form a new nation.

Page 49: 1. drop in at 2. hold his tongue 3. eyes 4. sit still under his wig 5. fly for his life 6. brains behind

Page 50: 1. England is making us pay a tax on everything that's printed! 2. A band of men just dumped a load of tea into the harbor! 3. The Redcoats are coming, and Paul Revere's spreading the alarm! 4. Sam Adams is in Philadelphia, and I hear he rode on a horse!

Page 51: Students' charts will vary, but should show basic ideas illustrated in the book.

Page 52: Students' Queue letters will vary.

Page 61: Students' words will vary.

Page 62: Students' riddles will vary.

Reading Motivators

DESK SIGNS

Reproduce, then cut out these pop-up desk signs for use with the unit. Present them to students upon completion of a book, and have students fill in their names. Instruct students to fold their desk signs in the middle and to cut the pictures along the dotted lines.

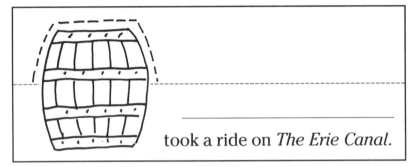

took a ride on *The Erie Canal*.

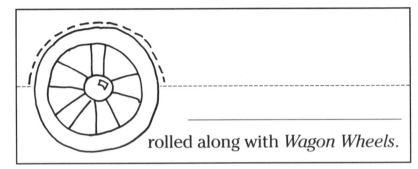

rolled along with *Wagon Wheels*.

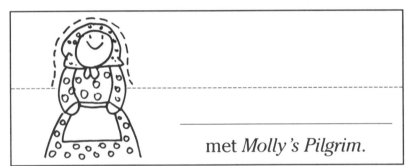

met *Molly's Pilgrim*.

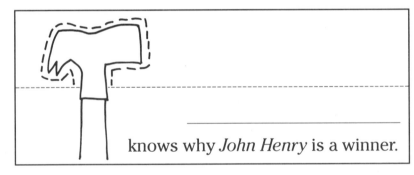

knows why *John Henry* is a winner.

galloped with *The Girl Who Loved Wild Horses*.

asked *Why Don't You Get a Horse, Sam Adams?*